AMERICA'S WILDERNESS

AMERICA'S WILDERNESS

...

The Photographs of
ANSEL ADAMS

With the Writings of
JOHN MUIR

COURAGE BOOKS
AN IMPRINT OF RUNNING PRESS
PHILADELPHIA · LONDON

© 1997 by Running Press
All rights reserved under the Pan-American and International Copyright Conventions
Printed in China

This book may not be reproduced in whole or in part, in any form or by any means, electronic or mechanical, including photocopying, recording, or by any information storage and retrieval system now known or hereafter invented, without written permission from the publisher.

9   8   7   6   5   4   3   2   1
Digit on the right indicates the number of this printing

Library of Congress Cataloging-in-Publication Number 96-69256
ISBN 1-56138-744-4

Cover design by Ken Newbaker
Edited by Elaine M. Bucher
Photographs researched by Susan Oyama

The photographs in this collection were reproduced from negatives of original Ansel Adams prints preserved by the National Archives. This book has not been authorized by and has no connection with Ansel Adams and the Ansel Adams Publishing Rights Trust.

Published by Courage Books,
an imprint of
Running Press Book Publishers
125 South Twenty-second Street
Philadelphia, Pennsylvania 19103-4399

CONTENTS

INTRODUCTION

"The charms of these mountains are beyond all common reason, unexplainable and mysterious as life itself."
—JOHN MUIR

The grandeur of the American landscape has captured the hearts and minds of many wilderness wanderers, filling them with the spirit of mountain woods. The sunlit mountain peaks and forest-clad hills have inspired artists and writers both to capture the beauty of nature and preserve her landscape for all to enjoy. Its mystery captured both the heart and the eye of one of the best-loved photographers and one of the most eloquent naturalist writers of the 20th century. Both Ansel Adams and John Muir were mesmerized by the beauty of the American landscape and, through their personal lives and their art, attempted to protect and preserve the source of their inspiration.

Ansel Adams's love affair with the American West began at an early age. In 1916, with his very first camera in hand, the 14-year-old Adams set off to explore Yosemite National Park and was captivated by what he saw. The natural wonders that lay in this park paradise became the subject of many of his later photographs. Traveling back to Yosemite each summer, Adams worked as a custodian of the Sierra Club Lodge and later as a guide for the club's treks through the park. While there, he cultivated his own photographic style, capturing the park land's glorious vistas and landscapes.

An accomplished wilderness photographer by the time he was 34, Adams was also an acknowledged master in the darkroom. In 1941, while teaching photography at the Art Center School in Los Angeles, Adams developed the "Zone System," a set of guidelines for planning the exposure and development of negatives. This innovation allowed Adams to control the contrasts of light and dark in his photographs and better capture his own vision of the landscapes he photographed. He went on to help found the department of photography at the Museum of Modern Art in New York, the first photography department at a fine-arts institution in the United States.

Driven by his desire to preserve the landscape he so admired, Adams petitioned Congress in 1936 for the creation of a national park in Kings River Canyon in California. Years earlier, William Henry Jackson had taken the first photographs of the Yellowstone area and the Mesa Verde cliff-dwellings in Colorado—photographs that influenced Congress to create Yellowstone National Park in 1872. Adams's portraits of snow-capped mountains and vast forests similarly convinced lawmakers of the need to protect and preserve the wilderness. Kings River Canyon was made a national park in 1940.

Happily, Adams's work also captured the eye of Secretary of the Interior Harold Ickes. In 1935 Ickes had begun a project to cover the walls of the new Department of the Interior museum with murals depicting the national park system. Numerous artists were commissioned, but no photographers. Photography was still viewed by many as a second-class art form. After viewing Adams's work, however, Ickes became convinced that his photographs captured both the beauty and the spirit of the American landscape. In 1941 he commissioned Adams to provide a series of photographs for the project.

Ansel Adams and the Mural Project were a perfect fit. The project gave Adams the excuse to visit and photograph the wilderness that he dearly loved and the opportunity to create a photographic record of the nation's park lands. Although the project was halted by the advent of the Second World War and the photographs were never used for their intended purpose, Adams contributed 225 prints that are now kept in the National Archives in Washington, D.C. The photographs in this collection were reproduced from negatives of original Ansel Adams prints preserved by the National Archives and represent approximately one-half of the pieces created by Adams during this period.

It is appropriate that the quotations accompanying these photographs are from the journals and essays of John Muir, a noted naturalist and explorer. Much like Ansel Adams, Muir crusaded for the establishment of national parks and the preservation of the American wilderness. Both Muir Woods National Monument and Muir Glacier are named in his honor.

Born in Scotland in 1838, Muir emigrated with his family to the Wisconsin in 1848. In 1868 Muir made his first trip to the Yosemite Valley, remaining there for six years. He became fascinated by the physical formations surrounding him and was among the first to demonstrate that the Yosemite Valley had been formed by glacial erosion.

Muir dedicated the latter portion of his life to the preservation of the Western forests that inspired much of Ansel Adams's work. He petitioned Congress for the National Park Bill establishing Yosemite and Sequoia national parks that was passed in 1890. When powerful lobbyists attempted to take away the forest reserves created by Grover Cleveland, Muir won public support through magazine articles advocating a national conservation policy. He founded the Sierra Club in 1892, a society for which Adams served on the board of trustees for 37 years.

The nation has changed dramatically since Muir and Adams enjoyed Yosemite. Our cities have grown tremendously, and civilization has invaded the American West. This collection, however, captures their vision of an Edenic world worth preserving. The pairing of Ansel Adams's photographs with the writings of John Muir is both powerful and eloquent. No one is more capable of understanding and giving voice to the wilderness images captured by Ansel Adams than Muir. Their vision, like the wilderness that they loved, is timeless.

SONGS OF THE EARTH

• • •

Some of the eternal beauty is always in
sight, enough to keep every fiber of us
tingling, and this we are able to
gloriously enjoy though the methods of
its creation may lie beyond our ken.
Sing on . . .

And oh! what streams are there! beaming, glancing, each with music of its own, singing as they go, in shadow and light, onward up their lovely, changing pathways to the sea. And hills rise over hills, and mountains, heaving, waving, swelling, in most glorious, overpowering, unreadable majesty.

Nature is ever at work building and pulling down, creating and destroying, keeping everything whirling and flowing, allowing no rest but in rhythmical motion, chasing everything in endless song out of one beautiful form into another.

The wildest geysers in the world, in bright, triumphant bands, are dancing and singing . . . amid
thousands of boiling springs, beautiful and awful, their basins arranged in gorgeous colors like gigantic
flowers; and hot paint-pots, mud springs, and mud volcanoes, mush and broth cauldrons whose contents
are of every color and consistency, splash and heave and roar in bewildering abundance.

An inspiration is this song of the blessed lark, and seems to be the only bird-song of these hills that has been created with any direct reference to us. . . . God be thanked for this blessed instrument hid beneath the feathers of a lark.

However perfect the season and the day, the cold incompleteness of these young lakes is always keenly felt. We approach them with a kind of mean caution, and steal unconfidingly around their crystal shores, dashed and ill at ease, as if expecting to hear some forbidden voice. But the love-songs of the ouzels and the love-looks of the daisies gradually reassure us, and manifest the warm fountain humanity that pervades the coldest and most solitary of them all.

What a romantic life this little bird leads on the most beautiful portions of the
streams. . . . No wonder it is a fine singer, considering the stream songs it hears day
and night. Every breath the little poet draws is part of a song, for all the air about the
rapids and falls is beaten into music, and its first lessons must begin before it is born
by the thrilling and quivering of the eggs in unison with the tones of the falls.

Think of this mighty stream springing in the first place in
vapor from the sea, flying on the wind, alighting on the
mountains in hail and snow and rain, . . . then gathering its
scattered waters, gliding from its noble lake, and going
back home to the sea, singing all the way!

How still the woods seem from here, yet how
lively a stir the hidden animals are making. . . . The
plants are as busy as the animals, every cell in a
swirl of enjoyment, humming like a hive, singing
the old new song of creation.

. . . the whole is enlivened and made glorious with
rejoicing streams that come dancing and foaming
over the sunny brows of the cliffs to join the
shining river that flows in tranquil beauty down
the middle of each one of them.

Even the blind must enjoy these woods, drinking their fragrance, listening to the music of the winds in their grooves, and fingering their flowers. . . . The kind of study required is as easy and as natural as breathing.

After gaining the open summit, . . . feeling the natural exhilaration due to the slight elevation of a thousand feet or so, and hopes excited concerning the outlook to be obtained, a magnificent section . . . came in full sight—a glorious wilderness that seemed to be calling with a thousand songful voices.

The network of dry water-courses, spread over valleys and hollows, suddenly gushes with bright waters, sparkling and pouring from pool to pool, like dusty mummies risen from the dead and set living and laughing with color and blood.

Every bird song, wind song, and tremendous storm song of the rocks in the heart
of the mountains is our song, our very own, and sings our love.

WANDERERS

...

The clearest way into the universe is through a forest wilderness.

But wheresoever we may
venture to go in all this good
world, nature is ever found
richer and more beautiful than
she seems, and nowhere may
you meet with more varied
and delightful surprises than in
the byways and recesses of
this sublime wilderness.

Wander here a whole summer, if you
can. Thousands of God's wild
blessings will search you and soak you
as if you were a sponge, and the big
days will go by uncounted.

Most travelers content themselves with what
they may chance to see from car-windows,
hotel verandas, or the deck of a steamer . . .
clinging to the battered highways like
drowning sailors to a life raft.

Somehow most of these travelers seem to care but little for the glorious objects about them, though enough to spend time and money and endure long rides to see the famous valley. But when they are fairly within the mighty walls of the temple and hear the psalms of the falls, they will forget themselves and become devout. Blessed, indeed, should be every pilgrim in these holy mountains!

When an excursion into the woods is proposed, all sorts of dangers are imagined. . . . Yet it is far safer to wander in God's woods than to travel on black highways or to stay at home. . . . No American wilderness that I know of is so dangerous as a city home "with all the modern improvements." One should go into the woods for safety, if for nothing else.

. . . its marvelous beauty, displayed in striking and alluring forms, woos the admiring wanderer on and on, higher and higher, charmed and enchanted.

The grandeur and inexhaustible beauty of each block would be so vast and over–satisfying that to choose among them would be like selecting slices of bread cut from the same loaf. . . . We readily perceive that this . . . is one batch of bread—one golden cake—and we are loath to leave these magnificent loaves for crumbs, however good.

A little higher, almost at the very head
of the pass, I found the blue arctic daisy
and purple-flowered bryanthus, the
mountain's own darlings, gentle
mountaineers face to face with the sky,
kept safe and warm by a thousand
miracles, seeming always the finer and
purer the wilder and stormier their homes.

We crossed the rugged,
picturesque basins . . .
full of beautiful cascades
and falls, sheer and
slanting, infinitely varied
with broad curly foam
fleeces and strips of
embroidery in which
the sunbeams revel.

How deep our sleep last night in the
mountain's heart, beneath the trees and the
stars, hushed by solemn-sounding waterfalls and
many soothing voices in sweet accord
whispering peace! And our first pure mountain
day, warm, calm, cloudless—how immeasurable
it seems, how serenely wild!

. . . the river issues from the north side in a broad, smooth,
stately current, silently gliding with such serene majesty that
one fancies it knows the vast journey of four thousand miles
that lies before it, and the work it has to do.

No matter how far you have wandered . . . the Grand Canyon of the Colorado,
will seem as novel to you, as unearthly in the color and grandeur and quantity of its
architecture, as if you had found it after death, on some other star; so incomparably
lovely and grand and supreme is it above all the other canyons in our fire-molded,
earthquake-shaken, rain-washed, wave-washed, river and glacier sculptured world.

Though of such stupendous depth, these famous canyons are not raw, gloomy, jagged-walled gorges, savage and inaccessible. With rough passages here and there they still make delightful pathways for the mountaineer, conducting from the fertile lowlands to the highest icy fountains, as a kind of mountain streets full of charming life and light, graded and sculptured by the ancient glaciers, and presenting, throughout all their courses, a rich variety of novel and attractive scenery, the most attractive that has yet been discovered in the mountain ranges of the world.

While traveling southward . . . I noticed a remarkably tall and imposing column, rising like a lone pine out of the sage-brush on the edge of a dry gulch. . . . It seemed strangely out of place in the desert, as if it had been transported entire from the heart of some . . . town and left there by mistake.

In so wild and so beautiful a region was spent my first day, every sound and sight inspiring, leading one far out of himself, yet feeding and building up his individuality.

Lakes are seen gleaming in all sorts of places—round, or oval, or square, like very mirrors; others narrow and sinuous, drawn close around the peaks like the silver zones, the highest reflecting only rocks, snow, and the sky. But neither these nor the glaciers, nor the bits of brown meadow and moorland that occur here and there, are large enough to make any marked impression upon the mighty wilderness of mountains. The eye, rejoicing in its freedom, roves about the vast expanse, yet returns again and again to the mountain peaks.

I feel eager and ready for another excursion a month or two long in the same wonderful wilderness. Now, however, I must turn toward the lowlands, praying and hoping Heaven will shove me back again.

Life seems
neither long
nor short, and
we take no more
heed to save
time or make
haste than do
the trees and
stars. This is true
freedom . . .

OUR
JOURNEY
HOME

• • •

Going to the woods is going home . . .

To lovers of the wild, these mountains are not a hundred
miles away. Their spiritual power and the goodness of
the sky make them near, as a circle of friends.

The scenery, too, and all of nature . . . is fairly enchanting.
Strange and beautiful mountain ferns are there, low in the
dark canyons and high upon the rocky sunlit peaks;
banks of blooming shrubs, and sprinklings and gatherings
of garment flowers, precious and pure as ever enjoyed
the sweets of a mountain home.

To . . . people from corn and cattle and wheat–field countries the canyon at first sight seems as uninhabitable as a glacier crevasse, utterly silent and barren. Nevertheless it is the home of a multitude of our fellow–mortals, men as well as animals and plants.

Centuries ago it was inhabited by tribes of Indians, who, long before Columbus saw America,
built thousands of stone houses in its crags, and large ones . . . on the mesas of the adjacent
regions. Their cliff-dwellings, almost numberless, are still to be seen in the canyon,
scattered along both sides from top to bottom and throughout its entire length,
built of stone and mortar in seams and fissures like swallows' nests.

We are now in the mountains and they are in us, kindling enthusiasm, making every nerve quiver, filling every pore and cell of us. Our flesh-and-bone tabernacle seems transparent as glass to the beauty about us, as if truly an inseparable part of it, thrilling with the air and trees, streams and rocks, in the waves of the sun—a part of all nature, neither old nor young, sick nor well, but immortal. . . . How glorious a conversion, so complete and wholesome it is, scarce memory enough of old bondage days left as a standpoint to view it from! In this newness of life we seem to have been so always.

When at length we enter the mountain gateway,
the somber rocks seem aware of our presence, and
seem to come thronging closer about us, . . . enabling
us to feel something of Nature's love even here,
beneath the gaze of her coldest rocks.

You can feel yourself out of doors; plain, sky, and mountains ray beauty which you feel. You bathe in these spirit-beams, turning round and round, as if warming at a campfire. Presently you lose consciousness of your own separate existence: you blend with the landscape, and become part and parcel of nature.

The charms of these mountains
are beyond all common reason,
unexplainable and mysterious
as life itself.

. . . we can see into the lower end of the famous valley, with it's wonderful cliffs and groves, a grand page of mountain manuscript that I would gladly give my life to be able to read. How vast it seems, how short human life when we happen to think of it, and how little we may learn, however hard we try!

As the night advanced the mighty rock walls of my mountain mansion seemed to come nearer, while the starry sky in glorious brightness stretched across like a ceiling from wall to wall, and fitted closely down into all the spiky irregularities of the summits.

Here every day is a holiday, a jubilee ever sounding with
serene enthusiasm, without wear or waste or cloying
weariness. Everything rejoicing. Not a single cell or crystal
unvisited or forgotten.

I only went out for a walk, and finally concluded to stay out
until sundown, for going out, I found, was really going in.

CIVILIZATION

• • •

Man is the most dangerous enemy of all . . .

Any fool can destroy trees. They cannot run away; and even if they could, they would be destroyed— chased and hunted down as long as fun or a dollar could be got out of their bark hides. . . . God has cared for these trees, saved them from drought, disease, avalanches, and a thousand straining, leveling tempests and floods; but he cannot save them from fools.

It appears, therefore, that notwithstanding our forest
king might live on gloriously in Nature's keeping,
it is rapidly vanishing before the fire and steel of man; and
unless protective measures be speedily invented and applied,
in a few decades, at the farthest, all that will be left
. . . will be a few hacked and scarred monuments.

On my last visit, as I was sauntering along . . . I was startled by a human track, which I at once saw belonged
to some shepherd. . . . Returning from the glaciers shortly afterward, my worst fears were realized.
A trail had been made down the mountain-side from the north, and all the gardens and meadows were destroyed
by a horde of hoofed locusts, as if swept by a fire. The money-changers were in the temple.

The dim old ruins . . . have something pleasing about them,
whatever their historical associations; for they . . . lend some
beauty to the landscape. Their picturesque towers and
arches seem to be kindly adopted by nature. . . . They have
served their time, and like the weather-beaten mountains
are wasting harmoniously.

In the settlement and civilization of the country, bread more than timber or beauty was wanted; and in the blindness of hunger, the early settlers, claiming Heaven as their guide, regarded God's trees only as a larger kind of pernicious weeds, extremely hard to get rid of.

Man . . . is making many far-reaching changes. This
most influential half animal, half angel is rapidly multiplying
and spreading, covering the seas and lakes with ships,
the land with huts, hotels, cathedrals, and clustered
city shops and homes, so that soon, we may have to go
even farther . . . to find a good solitude.

When I arrived at the village about sundown, the good people bestirred themselves, pitying my bedraggled condition as if I were some benumbed castaway snatched from the sea, while I, in turn, warm with excitement and reeking like the ground, pitied them for being dry and defrauded of all the glory that Nature had spread around them that day.

. . . to get all this into words is a hopeless task. The leanest sketch of each figure would take a whole chapter. Nor would any amount of space, however industriously scribbled, be of much avail. To defrauded town toilers, parks in magazine articles are like pictures of bread to the hungry. I can write only hints to incite good wanderers to come to the feast.

These imposing ruins . . .
present a most vivid picture of
wasted effort. Coyotes now
wander unmolested through the
brushy streets and of all the
busy throng that . . . spent their
time . . . here only one man
remains—a lone bachelor with
one suspender.

Thousands of
tired, nerve-shaken,
over-civilized
people are
beginning to find
out that going to
the mountains is
going home; that
wilderness is a
necessity; and that
mountain parks
and reservations are
useful not only as
fountains of timber
and irrigating
rivers, but as
fountains of life.

THE
SKY
ABOVE

• • •

The winds were hushed, the tundra glowed in creamy golden sunshine, and the colors of ripe foliage
of the heathworts, willows, and birch—red, purple, and yellow, in pure bright tones—were scattered everywhere,
as if they had been showered from the clouds like hail.

Winds are advertisements
of all they touch,
however much or little
we may be able to read
them; telling their
wanderings even by their
scents alone.

The air is electric and full of ozone, healing, reviving, exhilarating, kept pure by frost and fire, while the scenery is wild enough to awaken the dead. It is a glorious place to grow and rest in; camping on the shores of the lakes, in the warm openings of the woods golden with sunflowers, on the banks of the streams, by the snowy waterfalls, beside the exciting wonders or away from them in the scallops of the mountain walls sheltered from every wind.

How gently the winds blow! Scarce can these tranquil air
currents be called winds. They seem the very breath of
Nature, whispering peace to every living thing.

The big, gray days are exhilarating. . . . The snow that falls
on the lower woods is mostly soft, coming through the trees
in downy tufts, loading their branches, and bending them
down against the trunks until they look like arrows,
while a strange muffled silence prevails.

How beautiful their pearly bosses! How well they harmonize
with the upswelling rocks beneath them. Mountains of the
sky, solid-looking, finely sculptured, their richly varied
topography wonderfully defined. Never before have I seen
clouds so substantial looking in form and texture.

The voices of the mountain were still asleep. The wind
scarce stirred the pine needles. The sun was up, but it was yet
too cold for the birds and the few burrowing animals
that dwell here. Only the stream, cascading from pool to
pool, seemed to be wholly awake. Yet the spirit of the
opening day called to action.

The sky clears, . . . and up comes the sun like a god,
pouring his faithful beams across the mountains and forest,
lighting each peak and tree, . . . clothing them with the
rainbow light, and dissolving the seeming chaos of darkness
into varied forms of harmony. The ordinary work
of the world goes on.

The weather grows in beauty, like a flower. Its roots in the ground develop day-clusters a week
or two in size, divided by and shaped in foliage of clouds; or round hours of ripe sunshine wave
and spray in sky-shadows, like . . . berries half hidden in leaves.

The ground sounds hollow underfoot, and the awful
subterranean thunder sakes one's mind as the ground is
shaken, especially at night in the pale moonlight, or when
the sky is overcast with storm clouds.

Along the river, over the hills, in the ground, in the sky, spring work is going on with joyful enthusiasm, new life, new beauty, unfolding, unrolling in glorious exuberant extravagance—new birds in their nests, new winged creatures in the air, and new leaves, new flowers, spreading, shining, rejoicing everywhere.

Now comes sundown. The west is all a glory of color
transfiguring everything. . . . The radiant host of trees stand
hushed and thoughtful, receiving the Sun's good-night,
as solemn and impressive a leave-taking as if sun and trees
were to meet no more.

I set forth in the exhilarating freshness of the new day, rejoicing in the abundance of pure wildness so close about me.
The stupendous rocks, hacked and scarred with centuries of storms, stood sharply out in the thin early light,
while down in the bottom of the canyon grooved and polished bosses heaved and glistened like swelling sea-waves,
telling a grand old story of the ancient glacier that poured its crushing floods above them.

Sunshine over all; no breath of wind to stir the brooding calm. Never before had I seen so glorious a landscape, so boundless an affluence of sublime mountain beauty. . . .

The sky was perfectly delicious, sweet enough for the breath
of angels; every drought of it gave a separate piece of
pleasure. I do not believe that Adam and Eve ever tasted
better in their balmiest nook.

All things were warming and awakening. Frozen rills began to flow, the marmots came out of their nests in boulder-piles and climbed sunny rocks to bask, and the dun-headed sparrows were flitting about seeking their breakfasts. The lakes seen from every ridge-top were brilliantly rippled and spangled. . . . The rocks, too, seemed responsive to the vital heat— rock-crystals and snow-crystals thrilling alike. I strode on exhilarated, as if never more to feel fatigue, limbs moving of themselves, every sense unfolding like the thawing flowers, to take part in the new day harmony.

In March, plant-life is more than doubled. . . . Toward the
end of this month or the beginning of April, plant-life
is at its greatest height. Few have any just conception of its
amazing richness. . . . Well may the sun feed them with his
richest light, for these shining sunlets are his very children—
rays of his ray, beams of his beam! One would fancy
that these California days receive more gold from
the ground than they give to it.

The earth has indeed become a sky; and the two cloudless
skies, raying toward each other flower-beams and sunbeams,
are fused . . . into one glowing heaven.

NATURE

· · ·

Earth has no sorrows that earth cannot heal.

None of Nature's landscapes are ugly so long as they are wild; and much, we can say comfortingly, must always be in great part wild, particularly the sea and the sky, the floods of light from the stars, and the warm, unspoilable earth, infinitely beautiful, though only dimly visible to the eye of imagination.

Nature's sources never fail. Like a generous host, she offers here brimming cups in endless variety, served in a grand hall, the sky its ceiling, the mountains its walls, decorated with glorious paintings and enlivened with bands of music ever playing. The petty discomforts that beset the awkward guest, the unskilled camper, are quickly forgotten, while all that is precious remains.

Nature chose for a tool not the earthquake of lightening to rend and split
asunder, not the stormy torrent or eroding rain, but the tender snow-flowers
noiselessly falling through unnumbered centuries, the offspring of the sun and
sea. . . . Contemplating the works of these flowers of the sky, one may easily
fancy them endowed with life: messengers sent down to work in the
mountain mines on errands of divine love.

Silently flying through the darkened air, swirling, glinting, to their appointed places, they seem to have taken counsel together . . . and nothing that I can write can possibly exaggerate the grandeur and beauty of their work.

So extravagant is Nature with her choicest treasures, spending plant beauty as she spends sunshine, pouring it forth into land and sea, garden and desert.

Valleys . . . may be regarded as laboratories and kitchens, in which, amid a thousand retorts and pots, we may see Nature at work as chemist or cook, cunningly compounding an infinite variety of mineral messes; cooking whole mountains; boiling and steaming flinty rocks to smooth paste and mush—yellow, brown, red, pink, lavender, gray, and creamy white—making the most beautiful mud in the world; and distilling the most ethereal essences.

Nature . . . like a blacksmith blowing his smithy fires, shoving glaciers over the landscapes like a carpenter shoving his planes, clearing, plowing, harrowing, irrigating, planting, . . . like an artist—ever working toward beauty higher and higher. Where may the mind find more stimulating, quickening pasturage?

The whole
landscape showed
design, like man's
noblest sculptures.
How wonderful
the power of its
beauty! . . . Beauty
beyond thought
everywhere,
beneath, above,
made and being
made forever.

. . . glaciers, back in their cold solitudes, work apart from men, exerting their tremendous energies in silence and darkness. . . . They brood outspread over the predestined landscapes, working on unwearied through unmeasured ages, until in the fullness of time the mountains and valleys are brought forth, channels furrowed for the rivers, basins made for meadows and lakes, and soil beds spread for the forests and fields that man and beast may be fed. Then vanishing like clouds, they melt into streams.

All the earth hereabouts seems to be paint. Millions of tons
of it lie in sight, exposed to wind and weather as if of no
account, yet marvelously fresh and bright. . . . The
effect is so novel and awful, we imagine that even a river
might be afraid to enter such a place.

. . . how fine it would be could I cut a square of the tundra sod of conventional picture size, frame it,
and hang it among the paintings on my study walls at home, saying to myself,
"Such a Nature painting . . . would make the other pictures look dim and coarse."

When we emerged into the bright landscapes of the sun
everything looked brighter, and we felt our faith in Nature's
beauty strengthened, and saw more clearly that beauty
is universal and immortal, above, beneath, on land,
in heat and cold, light and darkness.

Even the majestic canyon cliffs, seemingly absolutely flawless
for thousands of feet and necessarily doomed to eternal
sterility, are cheered with happy flowers on invisible niches
and ledges wherever the slightest grip for a root can be
found; as if Nature, like an enthusiastic gardener, could not
resist the temptation to plant flowers everywhere.

EDEN

• • •

. . . [it] is a paradise that
makes even the loss of Eden
seem insignificant.

The grand show is eternal. It is always sunrise somewhere; the dew is never all dried at once;
a shower is forever falling; vapor is ever rising. Eternal sunrise, eternal sunset, eternal dawn and gloaming,
on sea and continents and islands, each in its turn, as the round earth rolls.

Nearly all the park is a profound solitude. Yet it is full of charming company,
full of God's thoughts, a place of peace and safety amid the most exalted grandeur
and eager enthusiastic action, a new song, a place of beginnings abounding
in first lessons on life, mountain-building, eternal, invincible, unbreakable order;
with sermons in stones, storms, trees, flowers, and animals brimful of humanity.

Here you may learn that the miracle occurs for every devout
mountaineer, for everybody doing anything worth doing,
seeing anything worth seeing. One day is as a thousand
years, a thousand years as one day, and while yet in the flesh
you enjoy immortality.

And the dawns and sunrises and sundowns of these mountain days—the rose light creeping higher among the stars, changing to daffodil yellow, the level beams bursting forth, streaming across the ridges, touching pine after pine, awakening and warming all the mighty host to do gladly their shining days work. The great sun-gold noons, the alabaster cloud mountains, the landscape beaming with consciousness like the face of a god. The sunsets, when the trees stood hushed awaiting their good-night blessings. Divine, enduring, unwastable wealth.

The big river has just room enough to flow and roar obscurely, here and there groping its way as best he can, like a weary, murmuring, overladen traveler trying to escape from the . . . abyss, while its roar serves only to deepen the silence. Instead of being filled with air, the vast space between the walls is crowded with Nature's grandest buildings. . . . Every architectural invention of man has been anticipated, and far more, in this grandest of God's terrestrial cities.

Leaving the workaday lowlands and wandering in the heart
of the mountains, we find a new world, and stand beside the
majestic pines and firs and sequoias silent and awestricken, as
if in the presence of superior beings new arrived from some
other star, so calm and bright and godlike they are.

Divine beauty all. Here I could stay tethered forever with just bread and water, nor would I be lonely; loved friends and neighbors, as love for everything increased would seem all the nearer however many miles and mountains between us.

Their union with the valley is by curves and slopes of inimitable beauty. They were robed with the greenest grass and richest light I ever beheld, and were colored and shaded with myriads of flowers of every hue, chiefly of purple and golden yellow. Hundreds of crystal rills joined song with the larks, filling all the valley with music like a sea, making it Eden from end to end.

After dark, when the camp was at rest, I groped my way back to the altar boulder and passed the night on it—above the water, beneath the leaves and stars—everything still more impressive than by day, the fall seen dimly white, singing Nature's old love song with solemn enthusiasm, while the stars . . . seemed to join in the white water's song. Precious night, precious day to abide in me forever. Thanks to God for this immortal gift.

This I may say is the first time I have been at church in California, led here at last, every door graciously opened for the poor lonely worshipper. In our best times everything turns into religion, all the world seems a church and the mountains altars. And lo, here . . . is blessed cassiope, ringing her thousands of sweet-toned bells, the sweetest church music I ever enjoyed.

Benevolent, solemn,
fateful, pervaded with
divine light, every
landscape glows like a
countenance hallowed
in eternal repose; and
every one of its living
creatures, clad in flesh
and leaves, and every
crystal of its rocks,
whether on the surface
shining in the sun or
buried miles deep in
what we call darkness,
is throbbing and
pulsing with the
heartbeats of God.

Whatever special nests we make—leaves and moss like the marmots and birds, or tents or piled stones—we all dwell in a house of one room—the world with the firmament for its roof—and are sailing the celestial spaces without leaving any track.

CREDITS

The quotes by John Muir were excerpted by the editor from his many journals and essays, including *The Mountains of California, Our National Parks, My First Summer in the Sierras, A Thousand-Mile Walk to the Gulf,* and *Steep Trails*.

All photographs courtesy of the National Archives Still Picture Branch.

Front cover and p. 11: The Tetons—Snake River, Grand Teton National Park, Wyoming (Neg. #79-AAG-1)

Back cover and p. 5 (bottom left): Grand Teton National Park, Wyoming (Neg. #79-AAG-6)

p. 2: Long's Peak from Road, Rocky Mountain National Park, Colorado (Neg. #79-AAM-1)

p. 5 (top left) and p. 124: Church, Taos Pueblo, New Mexico, 1942 (Neg. #79-AAQ-1)

p. 5 (top right) and p. 62: Boulder Dam, Colorado, 1941 (Neg. #79-AAB-10)

p. 5 (center) and p. 36: Near Death Valley, California (Neg. #79-AAD-2)

p. 5 (bottom right): In Glacier National Park, Montana (Neg. #79-AAE-23)

p. 6: North Palisade from Windy Point, Kings River Canyon, California (Neg. #79-AAH-18)

p. 8: Going-to-the-Sun Mountain, Glacier National Park, Montana (Neg. #79-AAE-12)

p. 9: McDonald Lake, Glacier National Park, Montana (Neg. #79-AAE-19)

p. 10: St. Mary's Lake, Glacier National Park, Montana (Neg. #79-AAE-1)

p. 12: Old Faithful Geyser, Yellowstone National Park, Wyoming (Neg. #79-AAT-27)

p. 13: The Fishing Cone—Yellowstone Lake, Yellowstone National Park, Wyoming (Neg. #79-AAT-12)

p. 14: Paradise Valley, Kings River Canyon California (Neg. #79-AAH-23)

p. 15: Grand Teton, Wyoming (Neg. #79-AAG-3)

p. 16: Kearsage Pinnacles, Kings River Canyon, California (Neg. #79-AAH-7)

p. 17: Mt. Moran, Grand Teton National Park, Wyoming (Neg. #79-AAG-5)

p. 18: Long's Peak from North, Rocky Mountain National Park, Colorado (Neg. #79-AAM-16)

p. 19: Grand Teton, Wyoming (Neg. #79-AAG-2)

p. 20: Mountains—Northeast Portion, Yellowstone National Park, Wyoming (Neg. #79-AAT-8)

p. 21: In Glacier National Park, Montana (Neg. #79-AAE-2)

p. 22: Central Geyser Basin, Yellowstone National Park, Wyoming (Neg. #79-AAT-1)

p. 23: From Going-to-the-Sun Chalet, Glacier National Park, Montana (Neg. #79-AAE-7)

p. 24: Grand Canyon National Park, Arizona (Neg. #79-AAF-3)

p. 25: Moraine, Rocky Mountain National Park, Colorado (Neg. #79-AAM-2)

p. 26: Grand Teton, Wyoming (Neg. #79-AAG-11)

p. 27: Fountain Geyser Pool, Yellowstone National Park, Wyoming (Neg. #79-AAT-17)

p. 28: Canyon de Chelly, Arizona (Neg. #79-AAC-2)

p. 29: Near Grand Teton National Park, Wyoming (Neg. #79-AAG-8)

p. 30: In Rocky Mountain National Park, Colorado (Neg. #79-AAM-6)

p. 31: Grand Canyon National Park, Arizona (Neg. #79-AAF-9)

p. 32: In Zion National Park, Utah (Neg. #79-AAV-3)

p. 33: The large stalagmite formations and the onyx drapes above it, in the King's Palace, Carlsbad Caverns National Park, New Mexico (Neg. #79-AAW-11)

p. 34: Boaring River, Kings Region, Kings River Canyon, California (Neg. #79-AAH-25)

p. 35: Yellowstone Falls, Yellowstone National Park, Wyoming (Neg. #79-AAT-3)

p. 37: Mt. Moran and Jackson Lake from Signal Hill, Grand Teton National Park, Wyoming (Neg. #79-AAG-7)

p. 38: Grand Canyon National Park, Arizona (Neg. #79-AAF-26)

p. 39: Grand Canyon National Park, Arizona (Neg. #79-AAF-24)

p. 40: Rock and Cloud, Kings River Canyon, California (Neg. #79-AAH-13)

p. 41: Detail of formations in the Big Room near the Temple of the Sun, Carlsbad Caverns National Park, New Mexico (Neg. #79-AAW-23)

p. 42: Evening, McDonald Lake, Glacier National Park, Montana (Neg. #79-AAE-16)

p. 43: Center Peak, Center Basin, Kings River Canyon, California (Neg. #79-AAH-17)

p. 44: An Unnamed Peak, Kings River Canyon, California (Neg. #79-AAH-8)

p. 45: Fin Dome, Kings River Canyon, California (Neg. #79-AAH-6)

p. 46: In Rocky Mountain National Park, Colorado (Neg. #79-AAM-3)

p. 47: Long's Peak, Rocky Mountain National Park, Colorado (Neg. #79-AAM-13)

p. 48: In Glacier National Park, Montana (Neg. #79-AAE-4)

p. 49: Castle Geyser Cone, Yellowstone National Park, Wyoming (Neg. #79-AAT-2)

p. 50: In Glacier National Park, Montana (Neg. #79-AAE-24)

p. 51: Middle Fork at Kings River from South Fork of Cartridge Creek, Kings River Canyon, California (Neg. #79-AAH-26)

p. 52: Mesa Verde National Park, Colorado, 1941 (Neg. #79-AAJ-4)

p. 53: In Rocky Mountain National Park, Colorado (Neg. #79-AAM-11)

p. 54: Peak near Rac Lake, Kings River Canyon, California (Neg. #79-AAH-1)

p. 55: In Glacier National Park, Montana (Neg. #79-AAE-9)

p. 56: Long's Peak, Rocky Mountain National Park, Colorado (Neg. #79-AAM-10)

p. 57: Grand Canyon National Park, Arizona (Neg. #79-AAF-12)

p. 58: Mt. Winchell, Kings River Canyon, California (Neg. #79-AAH-9)

p. 59: Cliff Palace, Mesa Verde National Park, Colorado (Neg. #79-AAJ-7)

p. 60: Jupiter Terrace—Fountain Geyser Pool, Yellowstone National Park, Wyoming (Neg. #79-AAT-20)

p. 61: Zion National Park, Utah, 1941 (Neg. #79-AAV-4)

p. 63: Boulder Dam, Colorado, 1941 (Neg. #79-AAB-8)

p. 64: Transmission Lines in Mojave Desert, Colorado, 1941 (Neg. #79-AAB-3)

p. 65: Burned Area, Glacier National Park, Montana (Neg. #79-AAE-3)

p. 66: At Taos Pueblo, New Mexico (Neg. #79-AAQ-4)

p. 67: Flock in Owens Valley, California, 1941 (Neg. #79-AAL-1)

p. 68: Walpi, Arizona, 1941 (Neg. #79-AAS-1)

p. 69: Cliff Palace, Mesa Verde National Park, Colorado (Neg. #79-AAJ-5)

p. 70: Church, Taos Pueblo, New Mexico, 1941 (Neg. #79-AAQ-3)

p. 71: Acoma Pueblo, New Mexico (Neg. #79-AAA-4)

p. 72: Church, Acoma Pueblo, New Mexico (Neg. #79-AAA-5)

p. 73: Church, Acoma Pueblo, New Mexico (Neg. #79-AAA-3)

p. 74: Roaring Mountain, Yellowstone National Park, Wyoming (Neg. #79-AAT-10)

p. 75: Old Faithful Geyser, Yellowstone National Park, Wyoming (Neg. #79-AAT-26)

p. 76: Clouds—White Pass, Kings River Canyon, California (Neg. #79-AAH-24)

p. 77: Yellowstone Lake, Yellowstone National Park, Wyoming (Neg. #79-AAT-5)

p. 78: Grand Canyon from North Rim, Arizona (Neg. #79-AAF-14)

p. 79: Rocky Mountain National Park, Never Summer Range, Colorado (Neg. #79-AAM-7)

p. 80: Grand Teton, Wyoming (Neg. #79-AAG-4)

p. 81: In Glacier National Park, Montana (Neg. #79-AAE-5)

p. 82: Half Dome, Apple Orchard, Yosemite National Park, California (Neg. #79-AAU-1)

p. 83: In Glacier National Park, Montana (Neg. #79-AAE-9)

p. 84: Evening, McDonald Lake, Glacier National Park, Montana (Neg. #79-AAE-6)

p. 85: In Glacier National Park, Montana (Neg. #79-AAE-13)

p. 86: Yellowstone Lake, Mt. Sheridan, Yellowstone National Park, Wyoming (Neg. #79-AAT-11)

p. 87: St. Mary's Lake, Glacier National Park, Montana (Neg. #79-AAE-15)

p. 88: In Rocky Mountain National Park, Colorado (Neg. #79-AAM-14)

p. 89: From Logan Pass, Glacier National Park, Montana (Neg. #79-AAE-10)

p. 90: Mt. Brewer, Kings River Canyon, California (Neg. #79-AAH-10)

p. 91: Tetons from Signal Mountain, Grand Teton National Park, Wyoming (Neg. #79-AAG-9)

p. 92: Heaven's Peak, Glacier National Park, Montana (Neg. #79-AAE-17)

p. 93: In Glacier National Park, Montana (Neg. #79-AAE-18)

p. 94: Coliseum Mountain, Kings River Canyon, California (Neg. #79-AAH-19)

p. 95: In Rocky Mountain National Park, Colorado (Neg. #79-AAM-4)

p. 96: Saguaro National Monument, Arizona (Neg. #79-AAN-6)

p. 97: Corn Field, Indian Farm near Tuba City, Arizona, in Rain, 1941 (Neg. #79-AAR-1)

p. 98: Rocks at Silver Gate, Yellowstone National Park, Wyoming (Neg. #79-AAT-7)

p. 99: In Saguaro National Monument, Arizona (Neg. #79-AAN-1)

p. 100: Old Faithful Geyser, Yellowstone National Park, Wyoming (Neg. #79-AAT-25)

p. 101: Junction Peak, Kings River Canyon, California (Neg. #79-AAH-11)

p. 102: Long's Peak, Rocky Mountain National Park, Colorado (Neg. #79-AAM-17)

p. 103: Corn Field, Indian Farm near Tuba City, Arizona, in Rain, 1941 (Neg. #79-AAR-2)

p. 104: Peak above Woody Lake, Kings River Canyon, California (Neg. #79-AAH-14)

p. 105: Jupiter Terrace—Fountain Geyser Pool, Yellowstone National Park, Wyoming (Neg. #79-AAT-16)

p. 106: Grand Canyon from South Rim, Arizona, 1941 (Neg. #79-AAF-8)

p. 107: Two Medicine Lake, Glacier National Park, Montana (Neg. #79-AAE-20)

p. 108: Formations and Pool, large drapery formation known as the "Guillotine," and the pool in the King's Palace, Carlsbad Caverns National Park, New Mexico (Neg. #79-AAW-13)

p. 109: Fountain Geyser Pool, Yellowstone National Park, Wyoming (Neg. #79-AAT-18)

p. 110: Grand Canyon National Park, Arizona (Neg. #79-AAF-16)

p. 111: Grand Canyon National Park, Arizona (Neg. #79-AAF-23)

p. 112: Grand Canyon National Park, Arizona (Neg. #79-AAF-20)

p. 113: Court of the Patriarchs, Zion National Park, Utah (Neg. #79-AAV-1)

p. 114: In Rocky Mountain National Park, Colorado (Neg. #79-AAM-18)

p. 115: In Rocky Mountain National Park, Colorado (Neg. #79-AAM-12)

p. 116: McDonald Lake, Glacier National Park, Montana (Neg. #79-AAE-14)

p. 117: North Dome, Kings River Canyon, California (Neg. #79-AAH-5)

p. 118: Grand Sentinel Kings River Canyon, California (Neg. #79-AAH-2)

p. 119: Grand Canyon National Park, Arizona (Neg. #79-AAF-19)

p. 120: Pinchot Pass, Mt. Wynne, Kings River Canyon, California (Neg. #79-AAH-12)

p. 121: Yellowstone Lake, Yellowstone National Park, Wyoming (Neg. #79-AAT-6)

p. 122: Owens Valley from Sawmill Pass, Kings River Canyon, California (Neg. #79-AAH-21)

p. 123: Fountain Geyser Pool, Yellowstone National Park, Wyoming (Neg. #79-AAT-19)

p. 125: Formations, stalagmites in the Queen's Chambers, Carlsbad Caverns National Park, New Mexico (Neg. #79-AAW-17)

p. 126: Lichen, Glacier National Park, Montana (Neg. #79-AAE-22)

p. 127: Canyon de Chelly, Arizona (Neg. #79-AAC-1)